Echoes of identity

Lauryn Nadine Wyse

BookLeaf Publishing

India | USA | UK

Presentation by *BookLeaf Publishing*

Web: www.bookleafpub.com

E-mail: info@bookleafpub.com

ISBN: 9789360944605

First edition 2024

to love, in every form

ACKNOWLEDGEMENT

to the muse within, who whispers poetry into the silence of my thoughts, and to the diverse voices that shape the world we navigate, thank you for providing the raw material for these echoes.

PREFACE

In the verses that follow, you hold not just a collection of poems but fragments of my soul woven into the artistry of language. 'Echoes of Identity' is an intimate journey through the corridors of my poetic mind, a labyrinth of emotions that resonate with the rhythm of love, the echoes of heartache, and the triumphant symphony of self-love.

As a young black woman, my pen becomes a compass navigating the vast landscapes of identity, culture, and society. Each poem is a stepping stone in my journey—sometimes stumbling, often dancing—towards self-discovery. In these pages, I unravel the threads that weave the fabric of my existence, seeking to understand the echoes of my place in the world.

Love is both a muse and a battlefield, and within these lines, you will find the tender whispers of affection, the echoes of love and the resilience born from heartache. Yet, beyond romantic entanglements, this collection delves into the profound love affair with oneself—a journey of empowerment, acceptance, and the unwavering pursuit of authenticity.

This book is an invitation to walk beside me as I navigate the diverse landscapes of my identity. Through the verses, I hope to spark a resonance within you—a shared heartbeat, a mirrored reflection, or perhaps a whispered recognition of our common human experience. May these echoes transcend the pages and find a home in the chambers of your own heart, fostering connection and understanding.

Thank you for embarking on this poetic voyage with me. May the echoes linger, resonate, and reverberate, forging a bond between us in the shared language of poetry.

With heartfelt gratitude,
Lauryn

Lauryn's lens at 14 -
'Happy?'

Happy? We're not happy we are angry,
we are angry beings
angry at the world we have been given
angry at this society we live in
and you wonder why our generation is failing?
it is because we have so many expectations but
nobody to help us,
nobody to guide us,
to believe in us
we are not trusted, but made to act responsible
being told the rules, but not how to avoid
breaking them
we are living in a society where we are doubted,
looked down on
and hated,
yet expected to show respect
we lack knowledge because we are not taught
what we should know
we are taught subjects but not life lessons
and this is where we go wrong
because we have nobody to teach us right from
wrong,

then you blame the parents, but if we're talking
realistically what time do parents really have on
their children/teenagers nowadays?
none,
because they are taken away by having to put in
so much work so they can earn the right amount
of money to keep their family stable,
to help them survive,
they are working hard because it is so easy to
lose a job now,
but so hard to find a new one
they are working for the money that the
government doesn't even want to give them
it's like you spit on our names yet want us to
look up to yours
but the problem here is you,
you don't trust us and you're too ignorant and
scared to put us in charge,
to give us responsibility,
to let US put anything into our own community.
and that sh- is not cool
you expect us to be happy but that word is
nothing to many
it has no meaning, we are oblivious to it
because in our generation, there is nothing to be
happy about.

love is complex

love is complex, no it's not a contest
and you'll realise when you're in that race
that the only person you're chasing is you

love is kind, so when it hurts more than a few
times,
question whether you're blind
i've heard that love does that sometimes

love is complex,
no it's not a contest
so why are you running out of breath to get to
the finish line?

love should be graceful and timeless
you shouldn't have to worry about whether
you're spending time less
or if the time you've spent is enough
to maintain that level of love
so now you're here trying to make it up -

but love is timeless, it doesn't sit on our watch.

connections

connections
true reflections
feeling deeper than the surface
sparks
bringing light to the dark

Our song

Our flesh and bones,
we synchronised in harmony,
as if we had rehearsed the song sheet a thousand
times and we finally made our debut,
both knowing which key came next
soaring for those high notes,
we vibed to our tune, instrumental so beautiful,
adlibs of 'aahs' and 'oohs',
I don't think a remix could ever top it,
it was perfect
I can't believe I wrote a song with you.

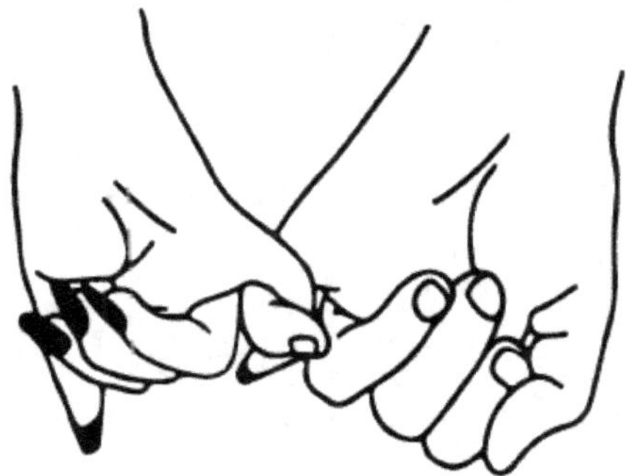

Lay down

When you finally make it home to me,
Can we just lay down?
Now and forever,
I need your love to wrap me like my warmest
sweater

I want to find comfort in your soul, let it speak to
me
Don't let the world lock you up, baby let's be free

I get scared of new connections, there's so much
temporary love and affection
I struggle to open up, when's the right time to hand
you the responsibility of my trust?

Searching for love in this world obsessed with trial
runs of lust, all these unfaithful stories have me
questioning the future of us

Swiping left or right like I'm searching for you in
the yellow pages, I want no part to play in these
new dating ages

I know the universe is going to bring you to me

So when you finally make it home, can we just lay
down?

polluted particles

polluted particles, intoxicated to the core
our bodies are dirty, our spirits are at war
people are taking their lives
morning, noon & night
living in a constant fear that things will never be
alright
viruses are spreading, bodies dropping like the
black plague
mistreatment of minorities, eyes opened to the
genocide in the USA
when the looting starts the shooting starts, a
clear pattern of who becomes prey
consumers of poison
addicted to the idea of better days
inebriated & injections
to numb away the never-ending pain
but you told your child that last time was the last
time you'd let them see you in that way again

even you can't comprehend, how you can wash
off these bloody stains

polluted particles, intoxicated to the core, our
bodies are dirty, our spirits are at war

i wish I could spark up some sage and that
would be enough to save us,
or have us all pray to our lord god saviours
restore some unity & have us all see that we are
in desperate need of some purity

invisible bruises, that never quite healed
we project our insecurities, then we put up our
shields

generational trauma, combatting our golden
dreams
outdated mindsets, living way beyond their
means,
holding us back, from a future serene

you can never really cleanse, if your water is
never clean

polluted particles, intoxicated to the core,
our bodies are dirty,
our spirits are at war.

what if

what if we never say what we feel?
what if we never know if it's really real?
what if our souls keep on crying?
what if the innocent keep on dying?
what if we never find our way?
what if the sun is forever overshadowed by the grey?
what if?
what if our roots become stray?
what if peace is overridden by affray?
what if
what if?

Brown baby (an ode to India Arie)

i love you auntie India
i love you auntie India for helping me love
myself

i love you auntie India for teaching me that i am
not my hair,
but that the 4c jungle on my head is beautiful,
that I can find my magic between these roots

that my brown skin is beautiful and there's not a
damn thing that I could ever wish to do, to
change that

i love you auntie India for teaching me that my
strength is nothing to do with my length and that
even a bald head could never define my beauty,

and so I wrote a poem auntie India when all of
these things seemed so clear to me, and I wanted
to pass on the same message to my future me
so she can love herself internally and eternally

brown baby
i pray for you

and I pray that you'll see that you don't need to
fit their shoe
and that their standard of beauty does not define
you

i pray for you, brown baby
and I pray that the lighter shades don't make you
feel any less about yourself

and I pray that your 4C, shrinkage and curls
don't make you question yourself
and I know, brown baby
society hasn't been set up for us to look at our
reflection and love ourselves
but I'm trying to love me so that I can love you
and I can fight your battles through me before
you have to
when they tell you you're pretty for a black girl
you tell them you're inherently gorgeous
any negative comments
you just gotta ignore it
and love yourself for you
through and through
always remember
you are perfectly you.

the canvas

i want to paint you,
i want my paintbrush to somehow illustrate how
radiant you are to me,
if I mix the right colours then maybe,
just maybe they'll see the warmth that you bring
to my canvas,
how aesthetically pleasing you are to my eye.
why,
if I had the option I'd keep you put, in my room,
couldn't move,
you'd always be there
because just your presence alone eradicates my
worst fears
you're like my lucky charm,
i wanna keep you as a bracelet on my arm, a
tailor-made one for me,
couldn't buy you on the high street,
something like 24k of glistening gold, coming
like royalty
what a masterpiece
they'd understand how perfectly imperfect you
are,
how your eyes shine bright like the stars,
how sometimes I wish I could see past, but I
can't.
the glare,

the one where I can see a thousand thoughts
racing through your mind,
but you won't let me in there
why won't you let me in there?
i just want to be near
you've got me in my room screaming 'baby
come closer'
picturing our future
whizzing our kids around town,
sun blazing, top down
so when my paintbrush touches this blank piece,
i need the angles to reflect how you're always
right there
for me
each stroke so delicate,
they will understand that the universe had to
take its time to create you,
that there is no other artist than me
that can portray you
so please, let me paint you.

I wailed

I wailed
like a baby in need,
I wailed for my mother's touch
the only one who could install pure reassurance,
on that day,
my maker
I envisage that is how you would've needed me
and I wouldn't yet be ready.

every/body

15

everybody is tryna get by
find their why
their piece of mind.

beauty

there is beauty in beginnings
boldness in believing
that the best is yet to come
Breathe.

soul searching

crippled
expiry
question and causation
closure
can I ever understand
couldn't be true
paralysed
soul peaking through space
wondering where the world is
our world
look around
darkness
shaken
must be mistaken
this is not our final destination
move
keep it moving
see you in time
our bodies choosing

DNA

from the root to the shaft
my dna is imprinted,
curls, coils, swirls
how could I ever want this texture to be lifted?
you are so much the beauty in me
and those before me
and those before them
imagine all the patterns intrinsically created
from those heads.

a nappy love story

finding love in her was finding a new love for
self
a compartment unlocked that made me feel
more grounded in me
more rounded in me,
there was nothing you could tell me about my
nappy head that I haven't already accepted
and if you see something you don't like when
you look at it,
then baby that is just a projection of yourself
my coils and i are sitting comfortably
sometimes she disobeys me
but I know it's all love.

THE WORLD IS ON FIRE

THE WORLD IS ON FIRE
SCORCHING
SO I SCREAM
INTERNALLY
I BLEED
EXTERNALLY
I SHED
ALL THE SORRY PARTS OF ME
IN MY HEAD
I QUESTION
ALL I CAN DO TO APPEASE
CLOSE MY EYES AND BREATHE
WISHING IT WERE A DREAM
HOW CAN WE COME 'SO FAR'
YET THIS IS OUR REALITY
OUR DYING HUMANITY
PLEADING FOR PEACE
IS OUR NEW PROFANITY.

suffocation

suffocated by self
solemnly swear that this can't happen again
sitting on the edge of my own brain, ears on
standby
ready to power at any given moment
the end
will they take control?
write the story for me?
whilst i live in regret?
fear beating like my heartbeat
until the door bruk down dead
risky,
risks lead to failure
failure or learning?
i suppose you learn both ways
i have learnt already
and fear the further lessons that could confront
me
will I be silenced from my truth?
i feel that most days already,
i despise how the system operates
i despise being privy to the evils
knowing that the set up means not everyone can
win
i pray the lessons learnt support me

i accept my failings and downfalls,
boundaries need to be exercised and clear
opt out of that which is unproductive
learn to lead with confidence
conviction
know your why
your how
be clear about your purpose
purposes
ever-changing
you can only listen for so long
until your ears bleed.
praying for you
trusting you to do better
praying for better
for sense of self
for rest
rejuvenation
for loud authenticity
praying deeply
praying hard
breathe through it
you will always have spirit
no matter what
speak life into self
you are not your shortcomings
you are not your failures
your mistakes
you are human

flawed, like all
not meant to be perfect
but a trier, a doer
i pray you find the strength to do the work you
dream of
to create the life you really want
what is it then
that you really want?

HER

I see her
Fulfilled
Happy knowing she kept going until she
achieved
The road wasn't clear, rocky and questionable
But the desire was deeper
Connecting the dots of dismay
Wanting to get stronger with prayer
So she prays
She believes so strongly that she can achieve
With the powers that be

She
She wakes up early, enjoys setting the tone and
giving thanks
She is so grateful for all that is and is to come
She is ready to take on what the challenges of
the day may be
For she understands her strength and resilience
Whilst knowing that she cannot conquer all,
balance
She is kind and pure
She wants everyone to know that love is the
answer
Love cures all

Whilst she continuously figures out what that
means to her
Learning to love, in love
Always learning to love self
The radiation from that can warm a community
And then some
She fights, for her happiness
The things and people that bring her joy
She doesn't care if it doesn't get received as well
She just creates, freely
She creates because she knows that creation is
power and energy
The energy we must use to fuel our connection
She lets go of perfectionism
And still tries, makes an effort, accepting that
it's okay if it could be better
One day it will be, but great things take time
So the building blocks consistently are more
important
She pays attention to what drives her
And she feeds it
She lets go of self-limiting beliefs, doubt and
angst
She is radiant, her energy is magnetic
She works hard, because she knows that a free
spirit must learn to thrive off of structure
Structure creates action and Action Creates
Things
She is connected to the higher version of herself

Even though she is still becoming
The connection is what drives her
She knows that there is so much more to come
from her
If she believes
Believes that her higher self is so much closer
than she thinks
If she lets go and believes.

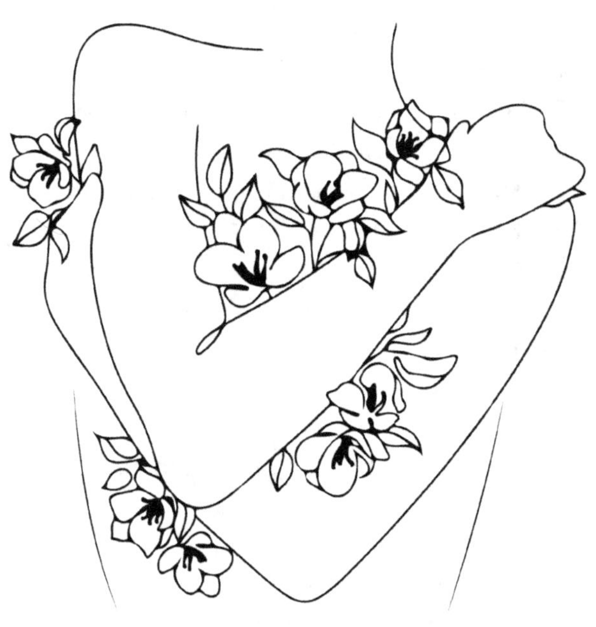

I am

i am your worst nightmare and your favourite
dream

i am everything you want me to be, but you say
you're still not ready

i am the moon in the midnight sky trying to
guide you on your way back home - but you stay
being lost

they say home is where the heart is,
but your heart is way too icy,
someone tell omarion he can take this icebox
back in a hurry

when I think you're about to say yes
you say no,
you let those clouded dark thoughts say 'I told
you so'
we need to beat them,
treat them,
show them that there's more to us than this

i need you to be on my team, you can't keep
forfeiting me on this
i am,

the atoms and the oceans,
the debris and the sunsets,
the particles and the pollution,
the product of everything and nothing,
the infinite,
a bonding,
the planets in the sky,
the soil beneath the concrete,
an energy,
a currency, i am all

i am everything you want me to be, but you say
you're still not ready

i say, I am.

self

in the midst of self-loving and self-destruction,
rewriting old pages and creating new chapters,
shedding old phases and singing new praises,
through it all I shine gracefully,
as a new version of self awaits for me,
we'll call this an evolution,
a transfusion of new knowledge and growth,
accepting mistakes and learning from
misfortune,
multitudes of cells refreshing and reproducing,
this feels like love,
but we're still on this journey,
in between the lines,
you can't comprehend this type of trip this early,
so hold on tight,
we're going on a trip
to our next chapter.

the reset

rewiring
rediscovering
recovering from the experiences that made me
for better or worse, I take my hand in marrying
myself in whole
wholeheartedly
whilst
remnants of past ridicule me
run, run
remind yourself that they are part of your story
story still being written
story still on the rise to revolutionary
story so early in its chapters you must remind
yourself
that although time is ticking
it is also a social construct
and up until the moment that you don't…
you have
all the time in the world
and that moment is one you will nearly never
know
so go,
flow
rebel against the clocks
tell them that your timing is perfect

that you know no such thing as too late
that the seasons await for you
and as long as you move
and keep on moving,
pace face, pace slow
you will know no such thing as out of time
because we are always
rewiring
rediscovering
retuning
from the experiences
that made us.